YouTube Marketing for Beginners

Growing Your YouTube Channel And Turning Your Subscribers And Viewers Into Profitable Customers For Your Business Through Selling and Affiliate Marketing.

Table of Contents

Introduction

Now more than ever more people want to start a YouTube channel. Whether it is to promote their business, have a daily vlog, stream gaming videos, host a cooking show – you name it – you can find it on YouTube.

However, with this high saturation of content, it is also becoming increasingly more difficult to get discovered and build a following. You can't just upload haphazardly and hope to get famous, this rarely leads anywhere except for a lucky few. You need to research your niche, understand filming and editing, how to interact with your viewers, and most of all, you need a game plan. The first step to success is knowing where you want to end up.

In this book you will learn the importance of YouTube, how to discover your niche, the basics of SEO marketing, the types of videos you can create, how to make an income, gaining a following, promoting your business, and more!

It may be a daunting start, but the important thing is to start. You might not be able to create a perfect channel from your first video, but even the most famous of YouTubers have cringe-worthy old videos. It takes practice to learn how to engage with your audience, what type of content to film, how regularly to upload, and more, but this book will help get you ahead of the curve and give you the knowledge and tools you need to improve.

Chapter 1: The Importance of YouTube

YouTube originally made itself known with cat videos and wacky, obscure content, but now it is the world's second largest search engine, second only to Google which owns YouTube. There are over a billion users, nearly one-third of everyone on the internet, and every day billions of hours of video are being watched. YouTube can be navigated in 76 different languages, that is 95% of everyone on the internet, and it is the second most visited website in the world.

Google prioritizes video content in its search results, especially video coming from YouTube. Website pages with video are 53x more likely to rank highly on Google searches.

It is plain to see why YouTube is a cut above other video sharing services with those statistics alone. If you want to get your name out there, it will go a long way towards helping you. However, why should you care about getting your name out there?

If you are a creative person, the answer might seem obvious, because you enjoy creating content whether makeup tutorials or video game streams and sharing it. But, if you are a business, the answer might be more difficult to see initially.

The beauty of YouTube for business is that it gives you a chance to get personal with your audience and gain their trust. For instance, say you run a small physical therapy business. You could produce videos on how to do a variety of exercises, thus setting yourself up as an authority on the matter and hopefully pulling in more customers.

It may seem counter-intuitive to teach your audience what

you want them to buy from you, but once they start learning from you, they will trust you and see the value you offer, making them more likely to use your business in the future.

YouTube also allows you to interact with your audience and customers. Try asking them questions in your videos, or if you notice people asking the same question frequently, you can make a video answering that question. You can comment on other people's channels, getting your name across their screen, which they will hopefully click if you are compelling. If you build that bond viewers become loyal, and it will also help you better understand whom your audience is, thus making you able to market yourself better.

If you want to make YouTube into a business, there are numerous options, from AdSense and affiliate marketing to ambassador programs and crowdsourcing. Just because it now takes longer to be able to use AdSense and make money that way, that doesn't mean there aren't other ways to turn it into a business.

YouTube is full of possibilities, whether you are using it for your business or want to make a business out of it.

Chapter 2: Learning Your Niche

You have decided you want to create a YouTube channel, the first question you should ask yourself is "what is my niche, what makes me special?" Sure, you could just start up a channel and post whatever ideas you come up with like most people do. However, time and time again this is shown to rarely work. Your viewers want to know what to expect from you, and the more specific you are, the easier it is to build an audience.

People can have a general daily vlog (video blog) where they talk about their life, but it still needs an angle. What about their life are people interested in, is it their job? Where they live? These types of vlogging channels are harder to gain a following on, but it is possible, and some people get lucky and quickly go viral off of one of their videos, resulting in a surge of new subscribers.

Find your niche, is it ketogenic cooking? Vegan makeup? Vehicle mechanics? Computer gaming? Try to narrow the field as much as you can to find your exact match, and then target that audience when creating your content. You want to make it clear who will be interested in your content.

After you discover what your niche is you need to do some research. Find what other people in that same niche are doing. You want to look at both the good and the bad. Try to learn from others mistakes, and look to see what the people with the most subscribers and viewer interactions are doing right. Take notes, really absorb everything you are learning. Don't just look at what they are doing on YouTube, but across all social media.

However, you can't do everything the same as those with a large viewership. For instance, they might not post regularly anymore, or they might have become slightly loose with what their niche is. They can do this because they already have a loyal following. But, when starting out it is really hard to build a following unless you begin with a firm foundation.

When researching your niche take note on what types of thumbnail they use, the length of their videos, what they talk about, how regularly they post content, how they interact with people both on and off of YouTube. You want to learn everything you can find. Once you know what works, you can learn how to adapt it to your own channel, and how to make your channel different from everyone else's and worth watching.

Not only do you want to study your competitor's technically well-done aspects such as thumbnails, editing, and lighting, but you want to ask yourself why their channel and individual videos do well. Why they are successful.

Once you know what makes your competition special, it's time to figure out what sets you apart, and how to take advantage of that. If you are a painter and want to share that with the world look at what other painters in the community are doing and what gap you can fill, maybe you could film watercolor painting tutorials featuring science-fiction and fantasy characters. If you are a baker, maybe your channel could focus on cupcakes or cookie decorating. If you are a gamer, maybe focus entirely on Overwatch or Minecraft.

You may think you want to keep your niche broad to attract a wider audience, but if you try to please everyone, you will end up pleasing no one. People want to hit the subscribe button to continue viewing videos within the niche you are offering. If one day you are posting tutorials, then an unboxing video, and then cat videos they won't know what to expect, leaving them confused and hesitant to hit that very important "subscribe" button.

There is one channel that does nothing but miniature foods and furniture for hamsters, yet they have had great success on YouTube doing this because they know their audience and they target a very specific subset of people.

Along with deciding on your niche you need to figure out what value you are adding to peoples' lives, why they should take the time out of their day to watch you. You could have amazing HD video, great editing, crystal clear sound, you could have it all, but if you aren't adding value to peoples' lives, then they won't care. Are you teaching them something? Making them laugh? Making them smile? Some gaming channels focus on teaching people and others that focus on making people laugh, both add value in different ways and attract different audiences.

Figure out in what way you want your channel to add value to peoples' lives, and then ask yourself if a video provides that each time during the production process. You don't just want consistent content, you want consistently *good* specific content.

In conclusion, it's important not only to have a niche but to know what that niche is and how to use it to your advantage, as well as how to make your videos impact your target audience.

- You need to be obsessed with your niche finding exactly what your audience is drawn to. Judge this by looking at the number of likes, comments, and subscribers the channel and videos have. The higher the more value and popular the niche and topic is.

- Don't just research your competition on YouTube. Look at blogs, Instagram pages, Twitter, Facebook, and forums related to your niche.

You want to have an edge over your competition in terms of the value and entertainment you're providing.

Finding problems and creating solutions works extremely well. I like to do my research for problems within my niche on forums, so typing in your keyword followed by "Forums – Advice Needed" will show you the language your audience speaks and what type of topics you need to dive into on your channel.

Remember:

- Decide your niche

- Research your niche (common keywords, thumbnails, titles, descriptions, etc.)

- Ask why the competitors' videos are successful

- Narrow down your niche

- Decide how you want to add value

- During production ask yourself if it fits your channel's niche

- Ask yourself if it adds value

Chapter 3: Creating a Name and Logo

When creating a channel name you want to think of it not as a single channel, but as a brand. How are you going to market yourself as a brand? You don't want a name such as Becky1990, you want a professional business name that you can utilize all across social media. Make sure that your channel name is available on all social media platforms and as a domain name, as well as not being copyrighted.

There are a few proven methods for choosing a marketable channel name:

- Use your legal name
- Use your niche in the name
- A combination of your name and niche

Your Legal Name:

Your legal name, either your full name or one of your names along with initials can be a wonderful way to brand not only your channel but yourself. It will make it easy for your followers to find you all across social media, and it looks professional. There are many people it has worked for, such as Tai Lopez, Grant Cardone, and Ingrid Nilsen, to name a few.

If you want to brand yourself, and not just your YouTube, this is a wonderful option. However, if you have a name that is difficult to spell make sure when you tell people your channel name that you also spell it out so that they can more easily find you.

A Niche Name:

Another wonderful option is to have a name that incorporates what your niche is so that people know what type of content you produce just by hearing the name. Some wonderful examples are Vlog Brothers, Geek and Sundry, Miss Orchid Girl, and Play Overwatch. Just hearing those names you have a general idea of what type of content those channels produce, and it also helps you remember their name.

Look around YouTube and Google to see if your idea of a name is taken. If you want to do a fitness channel, for instance, you want to make sure your channel name isn't overly similar to someone else's, especially if they are a large channel, as it will make it harder for people to find your content.

Niche + Legal Name

Names such as iJustine or Angel Wong's Kitchen are a success, because not only are they branding themselves by using their own name, but they also include their niche. The "i" in iJustine works, because it is referencing Apple's famous products, letting you know she is a tech channel. You know who Angel Wong is and that she produces a cooking show upon hearing her channel name.

Names such as this often work when they rhyme or start with the same letter, as well. For instance, if your name is Finn you could name your channel Finn's Fitness, or if you want to create a channel reviewing and brewing your own beer you could name it Beverly's Brews.

Logo Designs

Once you know your brand name, it's time to decide on a logo. Designing a specific logo enables you to build brand awareness and make it easier for your audience to remember you so that when people scroll past your profile, they remember exactly who you are. If you do not have a logo yet, you can consider getting one made by a freelancer on Fiverr, Upwork, or 99 designs. Fiverr and Upwork tend to run on the cheaper side of things, allowing you to get your logo from $5-$10. On the other side, 99 designs is more expensive, but it does allow you the opportunity to get a wide range of designs to choose from, and they tend to give outputs with higher quality.

Some things to keep in mind with your logo is not to use too many fonts. If you use more than two, your logo will look busy and messy. You also want an easy-to-read font that looks professional, no Comic Sans. Don't use a logo that requires color to get its message across, because there are instances, such as with watermarks, that you will want it to be a single color. When you do use a logo that has colors, make sure that the colors are easy on the eyes and blend well together.

The logo and channel name may not seem important, but first impressions mean everything. You want something that gets your message across and helps you market yourself professionally.

Chapter 4: Types of Content

Within a niche, there are many types of content you can create – you have to decide what fits your brand and personality the best. Sometimes you can do multiple types of videos, but try to keep it to one to three types, so that your audience knows what to expect from you. For instance, iJustine mostly focuses on unboxing and educational content about technology on her channel, but due to demand from her audience, she will also include vlogs going about her life or chronicling her kitchen mishaps from time to time. While she does more than one type of content, people know what to expect from her because she is still limiting it.

There are many types of video content, but the majority fall within these categories:

Vlogs

A vlog, or a video blog, chronicles a person's life. Some people choose to only do a couple vlogs a week, while others choose a daily vlog. While vlogs are a wonderful option, you usually see a slower increase in subscribers than in the other types of content. However, they tend to foster a sense of community.

Educational

One of the wonderful things about the internet is the ability to learn almost anything, and YouTube is front and center in the options for learning. Many people have a hard time reading long articles on a given subject, and can more easily learn through audio and visuals. Whether you want to teach people how to cook or how to use Photoshop, educational content is a wonderful option that can gain a large audience.

Product Reviews

People enjoy knowing that the products they are buying are trustworthy, making product reviews a highly sought after form of content. Technology reviews are especially popular. However, they are only successful when you have gained the trust of your audience, and they know you will tell them the truth if you dislike a product, even if you are being paid to review the product.

Q&A

Doing the occasional questions and answers video is a great way to interact with your audience, to make them feel heard and help them get to know you better. It's a good way to connect and build a loyal following.

Interviewing

You can interview people in your niche and ask about their journey. This works better for when you have a larger following because you will get more people saying yes if they see you have a large following. If you want to do this in the early days, you're best to interview channels that are on a similar amount of subscribers so you can help each other build at the same time.

Extra Types of Videos for Fun

Gaming

According to a recent study of gaming channels – usually involving a person streaming themselves gaming along with voice and sometimes filming themselves with a camera simultaneously – revealed they have a 15% higher chance of succeeding on YouTube than other types of content. With the many types of gaming platforms and games out there, the options are vast.

Animals

YouTube was originally known in part for cute animal videos, and that still has not changed. There are some great pet channels out there such as Stormy Rabbits, Milo Meets World, and Jessica Coker and her pet fox Juniper. They are all good examples of how to share quality animal content that keeps people coming back for more.

Beauty

Beauty videos are incredibly popular. This category often reviews makeup brands and shows how to create different "looks" with makeup, hair, and fashion. There are many top beauty gurus on YouTube, but Zoella and Jackie Aina are two wonderful examples of this category.

Comedy/Sketch/Parodies

Everyone loves to laugh, and YouTube provides a wonderful opportunity for many comedians to share the art of humor. Drew Lynch, who was once on America's Got Talent, now makes his living by sharing his humor on YouTube.

Shopping Hauls

People love shopping hauls, they almost always end up ranking well in terms of views. Shopping haul videos can help the viewer participate in the fun of the shopping experience without actually spending any money. Many people will also use them as inspiration for what they do want to buy.

Unboxing videos

Similar to shopping hauls and product reviews, but slightly different, unboxing videos are typically someone's first impression as they open a new product. Technology products, such as computers or smartphones, tend to do well in this category, especially when it is a newly released item. People love getting a look at a product as soon as it is made available.

Pranks

There are some huge prank channels, but this also comes with a word of caution. Many pranks can end up harming the person being pranked either physically or emotionally and can leave the prankster in hot water. It can be difficult to come back from a prank gone bad. If you choose to go the pranking route be careful.

Memes/Tags

Various tags go viral, for instance, the "what's in my bag" tag is popular in both the beauty and the vlogger/lifestyle sectors. It can be fun to join in on the tag that is currently going around and be a part of the community, but it can also help you network with others in your niche and help more people discover your channel.

Best Of/Favorites

People love watching "Best Of" and "Favorite" videos. For instance, "Best Computers of 2018," "Top 5 Favorite Lipsticks," or "The Best 10 Books of 2017." Not only are these types of videos entertaining, but they help educate the viewer and give them the knowledge to know what they want to buy on any given topic.

There are many types of videos you can produce, and once you know your niche, it can be easier to decide what type of content fits your brand. If your brand is stunning makeup on a budget then the beauty, product reviews, and occasional Q&A could be a great fit for you. Look at your favorites and top influencers in your niche and see what they are doing for inspiration.

Using YouTube without showing your face

This can be done of course. There are things to consider but if you want to own a brand or already have a brand that's driven through a Penn name or your niche is mainly about providing information then you can create YouTube videos without showing your face.

This isn't recommended because engaging with your audience on a personal level create trust and trust is what will build your following and ultimately drive your subscribers to become customers for your business.

YouTube Video Recording

When filming you first want to make sure you are in a good energetic mood. If you are excited about the content you are sharing it will help your audience be excited as well. This means you want to not only show in your body language that you are excited but in your voice as well.
If your pitch is low and your speech is slow it will bore the viewer, but if you keep your voice light and excited it will help your audience stay interested and hooked on what you are saying.

Be sure that while you are doing this you are also providing value to your viewer, you may be nervous about filming and it may be awkward. But, remember that practice makes perfect. Your viewers won't care if you come across as perfect as long as your content provides value and you are delivering the content you promised in the title. Not only will your audience be happy as long as you are adding value, but over time you will become more comfortable and it will no longer feel awkward.

While professional camera options are wonderful, they are not needed. Your audience will be perfectly happy with recordings from your smartphone, as long as you are providing value. You provide this value by giving them the information they need, by being true to the title of your video, and they won't even notice that the video was recorded using a phone.

Chapter 5: Producing Quality Content and Video

When people watch a professional channel, they expect high-quality content. Even if you have figured out your niche and produce good videos, if the technical aspects are of poor quality then people are usually going to leave. People don't want to stick around for a video with bad sound or a shaky camera. However, if you have a smartphone like an iPhone or Samsung, this is good enough to start with.

Generating Content Ideas

When starting out one of the most important things is to post new content consistently. If your viewers have no idea when you will be around, or if you will ever post again, they are unlikely to subscribe. It is best to try to post at least once a week, but two to three times is even better. However, you have to make sure all of this content is top notch.

One of the best ways to come up with content plans is with mind mapping. This is where you write a category, and then around that category, you will write related topics. You can get more and more detailed with each category, helping you create content ideas. For instance:

- Dangers of Declawing

- Top 10 treats

- The best toys

- Introducing your dog to strangers

- Training your dog not to jump on you

- What foods your dog should never eat

- Introducing your cat to a new cat

- Cats: How often your cat needs a checkup

- Top 10 best family dog breeds

- Dogs: Hypoallergenic dog breeds

- Raw Food or Kibble

- Best rated flea products

- Hunter Instincts

- Feeding your dog a raw diet

- Caring for your dog during the heat of summer

- Introducing your dog to a new cat

- How to make Homemade Cat Food

As you can see, mind mapping can help you come up with an abundance of ideas. They may not all be ready to film from the start, but if you work at them, they can become top-notch videos.

While it's a good idea to write bullet points of topics you want to talk about in your video, you shouldn't create a word-for-word script, because people will see you are scripted and feel as though you are fake.

Lighting

To get a proper video, you need good lighting. Ideally, you could buy some professional photography lights, reflection boards, maybe a ring light. However, these are not necessities. While these do help you have good lighting any time of the day and anywhere, just having a well-lit environment either outdoors or indoors in front of a window can be enough. Just keep in mind that this won't work at night or on cloudy days.

Sound

There are some wonderful microphones out there that can connect to either your smartphone or camera. The ones that attach to your camera tend to either need to be hooked up to your computer or to a powers supply/adapter. This can sometimes be really important if your camera or phone doesn't pick up sound very well. However, if you can get pretty clear sound from your camera, you should be okay.

It's important to remember when filming in noisy environments that once recorded it will be a lot harder to hear your voice than you expected. Windy environments are also not friendly to microphones as it causes a loud blotchy sound that will cover up anything else.

Filming

Nowadays most smartphones have HD video, so while a nice camera will greatly improve your video, if you don't have one there is no need to worry. Get started with what you have, and you can upgrade later. However, if you do want to get a nice camera the difference will show, some good choices are Canon EOS Rebels, Canon PowerShot G7 X Mark II, Fujifilm X-A5, GoPro Hero6 Black, and Nikon D5600. All of these cameras boast different features, but they will all provide high-quality video for your filming needs.

If your filming requires sharing your computer screen Open Broadcast Software, also known as OBS Studio, is a wonderful option that is free to use on Windows, Mac, and Linux.

You can either hold the camera or smartphone, prop it up on something eye-level, or use a tripod. To start filming, you will need to find the video setting on either your camera or smartphone and then just press "record." If you are filming on a camera, you will need an SD card, which you can then put into your computer to take the footage off of it. If you are filming on a smartphone, you can usually connect your phone to your computer with a wire and either take the files off directly or connect it to iTunes to get access to the files.

Music

Music is an important aspect of videos. While every video doesn't need music, those that use it effectively greatly enhance their videos. A couple instances where music helps is during scenic shots or any clip where you have the audio muted. However, you can't just use any music. For instance, if you used Taylor Swift, your video will be flagged for copyright infringement and removed. You need to find copyright-free music, and one great place for this is right on YouTube. If you go into Creator Studio, there is a section titled Create, and in that section is a subsection titled Audio

Library. There you can find music and sound effects that are free to use.

Editing

Most computers come with video editing software, such as Microsoft computers which come with Windows Movie Maker and Apple computers which come with iMovie. These are great easy-to-use programs, both for beginners and experts. You can also easily find tutorials for them online. However, if you want to get into some serious editing, you will eventually want to buy your own program that is more powerful. Sony Vegas Movie Studio is a wonderful choice that allows you to do almost anything and isn't overly complicated.

Headlines

You want to create headlines that pop, that create a sense of curiosity or wonder. However, at the same time, the headlines need to get the message of what your video is about across and be honest. Such a title would be "5 Makeup Trends You Need to Learn Today" or even "Emotional Trip to the ER." People are tired of click-bait, so make sure your headlines are genuine.

Thumbnails

First impressions are everything, and the first thing people see of your video is your thumbnail. YouTube will suggest three different automated thumbnail options, but these typically are not a good idea to use, as they are unoriginal and usually poor quality. You want to save a still from your video, which you can then edit in Photoshop, Gimp, or PicMonkey to make it look special and draw attention to whatever your thumbnail is about. Look at your competition to see how they edit their thumbnails for inspiration.

To upload a custom thumbnail (or schedule a video to publish at a specific time and date, for that matter), you must have a verified channel.

Closed Captions

To make good content, you need to make it accessible. Part of this is making it so that people with hearing disorders, who are hard of hearing, or who are Deaf can take part. YouTube is known for having terrible automated captions that do not convey what is actually being said, however, you can upload your own captions and then time it to the video. YouTube also has a feature to help you transcribe as the video runs. If you don't have the time to add captions yourself, you can hire someone you know or hire someone off of Upwork to help.

Not only do closed captions make your video more accessible, but adding them in also adds important keywords making it easier for search engines to recommend your video in relevant searches.

It may be daunting to create good content, but if you create a checklist and take it one item at a time you won't forget anything, and you can ensure your content is always as professional as possible.
While high-priced items may help you produce better videos, thankfully in this day in age it is possible to create decent content without the use of expensive equipment.

Creating Videos and Uploading Them to YouTube

To transfer files to your computer you can either remove the SD card from your camera and place it in your computer, then open up the file folder for the SD card and copy the files to your computer. If you are filming on a smartphone you can connect your phone to your computer with a lightning/USB wire or a micro USB/USB wire and either take the files off directly or connect it to iTunes to get access to the files.

You don't have to edit your videos. It can be a wonderful tool, however, it is possible to film them so that they don't need any editing. However, if you choose to edit your videos, while not required, you can use iMovie or Windows Movie Maker.

Uploading a video to YouTube is really easy. Open up the YouTube main page and along the top, you will see an upwards pointing arrow. Click on this arrow to go to the upload page, where you can select the video file that you previously edited. Once the video is uploading you can customize the headline, thumbnail, description, and tags.

Later on, if you want to make more changes to your video then click on your icon in the top left corner of the YouTube main page. A drop-down menu will display, and you will want to click Creator Studio. This is where you can find all the tools you need to manage your YouTube page. In the right-hand sidebar, you can find your "video manager," here you can go to individual videos to edit their captions, edit the video itself, or change any other information regarding your video.

Chapter 6: Building and Interacting with an Audience

While getting views is important, what will really help your channel is getting a loyal following? People who will stick around waiting for your next video, who comment and give you a "like," people who will share your content with their friends and family. In this chapter, we will go over not just how to get more views, but a loyal audience.

Keep Viewers Interested

Before you can build an audience, you need to keep your viewers interested. The first five to ten seconds of your video is the most important, this is when most people will click away to find a video that they think they will enjoy more. If you want to start your video with a logo or an opening clip, I urge you not to do this, as they will more likely click away.

Every video needs to start with a hook. Make the viewer see right away why they want to stick around, that you have the content that they want or need. If you want to use a logo or an opening clip, use it after the hook. Look at the popular channel *The Frey Life* as an example, they are daily vloggers who have turned YouTube into a business. While they do have an opening clip paired with music, they always first start out the video with a hook and *only then* add in the opening clip.

Part of having people stick around is being dynamic. If you just sit back and drone on in a low voice, your audience will start to get bored. However, if you show that you are happy or excited, both with your voice and your body language, your audience will feel that way too. But, you have to genuinely feel that way. If you are putting on an act or reading a script, your audience will feel that you aren't genuine, and it will turn them off from your channel. You want to have a personality, but not be a personality.

Another part of keeping people interested is staying active. If your audience sees you only post here and there, with no discernible timetable and no telling if you will ever post again, then they are less likely to subscribe. Try to post at least once a week, but two or three times a week is best as mentioned before.

When producing content try to think about creating binge-able videos. People often go to Netflix, Hulu, and yes, YouTube, to not just watch a single video but to watch many. When planning out your content set up a schedule to post videos that work well together, almost as if it were a TV series. If you post a video on how to bring home an adopted cat one day, then maybe later that week you could share a video on introducing a new cat to your other pets, and maybe the week after that you could share a video on choosing the right brand of cat food. Try to share content that not only works well together but that your viewers will see and go from one to the next binge-watching them.

Lastly, you need to make sure that the content you are providing is high-quality and up-to-date. If someone clicks on your video only to see that nothing about your content is fresh and new, they will leave.

Interacting on YouTube

YouTube isn't just a video sharing website, it is also a social media website. To be a part of YouTube you need to be social, to interact with both your viewers and other channels. This doesn't mean going to other channels and commenting "cool content, check out my channel," or "sub for sub," this is spam and will only raise the ire of the people who see it.

Try watching other peoples' content, and comment something of value to say, even if it is only a genuine "I really enjoyed your video, thank you for sharing." Over time this person might notice that you have an interesting channel name, that your avatar looks cool, or that they appreciate your adding value to their comment section and decide to check out your channel. And, not only will the owner of that channel see your comments, but anyone reading their comment section will see what you have to say and might decide to check your channel out.

When people comment on your content, it's important to interact with them. Once you gain a large following, you won't have time to reply to everyone, but still, let them know you are reading their comments by mentioning it in your videos or "liking" their comments. However, when you are starting out try to reply to everyone who posts a genuine comment. Answer their questions, thank them for watching, and tell them you hope they continue to enjoy your videos. You don't have to say a lot, but knowing that their comment was read and interacted with will make your viewers feel appreciated and special.

Draw People to Your Business

Whether you are using YouTube to promote your business or hoping to turn YouTube into your business, you need to draw your viewers to the business side. One quick and easy way to do this is to add a call-to-action at the end of each video. You do this by asking them to give your video a thumbs-up, to subscribe if they haven't already, to comment their thoughts, to check out your website or merchandise, or to follow you on other social media.

You don't want to go for the hard sell. This will turn people off, they don't want to feel as if they are just being sold something. First, give them the content and value they want, and then go for the soft sell with your call-to-action.

Getting Your Content Out There

When trying to promote yourself, it is important to not sequester yourself solely to YouTube. Share the content you are producing on Twitter, Facebook, Tumblr, LinkedIn, wherever you can think to share it. If you are filming out in public and someone asks you about it, don't just tell them it is for YouTube, tell them your channel name so they can check it out. Even better would be to have business cards made with your channel name that you can hand out to people who ask.

Tell your friends and family about your channel, they can be your biggest fans and support, especially when starting out. Word of mouth is a proven method for advertisement, and if your family and friends tell people they know about your channel, you will gradually gain a larger following.

A lot of people create articles around videos they have made on YouTube and post them on their blog and Facebook so their audience can read or watch their content revolving around the topic. This creates increased traffic to both your blog (if you have one) and, more importantly, your YouTube Channel.

Going Viral

There is wonderful solid content produced every day on YouTube, yet most of it doesn't go viral. There is not a formula to create a viral video. However, the videos that do go viral are usually innovative, exceptionally funny, or surprising. Look at the TwirlyGirl video that went viral. A small company produced the video and shared it on social media, and it went viral because it was funny, innovative, and it was directed towards their target audience.

If you are trying to build an audience, it is important to keep in mind who that audience is, what they enjoy and how to market your content specifically to them. Your audience wants you to be real and appreciate that they spend their valuable time watching and engaging with you. It may take time to build an audience, or you may get a surge of subscriptions overnight, but if you are patient and follow this advice the following you do get will be a loyal one.

Chapter 7: SEO and Branding

Branding is not only for companies, whether you hope to make a business out of YouTube or use it for a business you already have what you need to brand yourself. People need to know who you are and what to expect from you.

Branding

One simple way to brand yourself is to use the same name and logo across all of social media, this will make it easy for people to find you.

Try to keep the names and thumbnails across your videos looking consistent, you don't want to have one editing style for one thumbnail and a completely different editing style for another. Choose something so that when people see it, they immediately know it is you.

When titling your videos don't completely change the way in which you title them, for instance, don't title one "The Best 10 Hidden Restaurants in Los Angeles," and then title the next one "U Will NOT Believe What Happens!!! WATCH NOW!" For that matter, you never want a title like the second one. Make your brand recognizable.

When titling a video, you also don't want to start out with your company's name or "Vlog #5." You have little room to catch peoples' attention, so start with a catchy title that accurately represents what your video is about.

YouTube's end screen feature is another wonderful way to brand yourself. For five to twenty seconds YouTube will allow you to have links to other videos and subscribe buttons at the end of your video. This is a great opportunity to gain more subscribers and draw people to content you have previously produced. For your end screen, you can just have your logo for those five to twenty seconds, but it is even better if you are on the screen talking and making a call-to-action, asking people to click those buttons.

Part of branding is often showing your face, letting people know who it is behind the brand. However, that doesn't mean this is the only way. If you wish to remain anonymous you can produce content without showing your face, people can still come to trust you if they find your voice to be genuine, easy to listen to, and your expertise reliable. A good example of this is MissOrchidGirl.

Search Engine Optimization (SEO)

SEO may seem like a mysterious scary term, but there is nothing to be afraid of, it is not difficult to add some simple SEO features to your channel helping you get more views.
But, what is SEO? It is short for "search engine optimization." Put simply, you try to use keywords that search engines are most likely going to find you by so that you will be ranked higher in search results both on YouTube and on Google.

Keywords are important, they are what enables SEO to function. You want to fill your video titles, descriptions, tags, about page, everything, with keywords. Now, you can't just add a whole list of keywords, except in the tag area, you need to naturally use the keywords that relate to your brand while discussing it. For instance, if you have a gaming channel you could fill out your description with something like:

"Thank you for watching Gaming with Steve, I hope you enjoyed watching today's video on how to get better aim and more headshots on Overwatch. Don't forget to follow me on Twitch and Twitter to get updates as they happen."

Not only does this example include the channel name, but it includes the keywords "better aim" and "Overwatch." Now, when people search for improving their aim in Overwatch that video is more likely to rank highly. However, keep in mind that YouTube only shows the first one hundred or so characters of your description before making your audience click "read more," so you want to include any important call-to-actions or links at the beginning of the description.

Some people will add random keywords to their videos, however, this does nothing but annoys the viewer because the keyword wasn't related to the video, meaning the video isn't what they wanted. They will most likely just leave and find what they actually want, or they may even leave an angry comment.

If you add closed captions to your videos for accessibility those will also add to your keywords, helping your SEO.

Google Ads has a program, Google Keyword Planner, and this can help you find the best keywords to use for your specific content.

When creating keywords it is important to know the difference between short tail and long tail keywords.

Short tail keywords are broad and are three words or less, whereas long tail keywords are more than three words and are meant to target a very specific person. While short tail keywords can bring in a lot of viewers, it may or may not be that they are wanting. Short tail keywords will also provide a lot more competition, because if the keyword is "pizza" there will be a lot of other people ranking higher than you in the search results. Google AdWords also charges more for short tail keywords, as many people want them.

However, those who find you due to your long tail keywords will likely want exactly what you are providing, as you were specific when creating the keyword and you are less likely to have a large competition for the first-page search results. Overall long tail keywords are usually better. However, when possible, it is helpful to include short tail keywords as well.

Analytics

In the YouTube Creator Studio you will find a section titled "Analytics," and if you learn how to use this tool, your channel can grow greatly. How does analytics help? Using this tool, you can learn who is watching your videos, where they are from, what device they watch on, how long they watch for, how many views different videos get, and more! Using this you can find what your audience likes and tailor your content to fit them better.

While many people only focus on the number of views, what is actually more important is watch time. If you see that your viewers tend to only watch one minute of your shopping videos but watch seven minutes of review videos, you will know what type of content you should and shouldn't create.

If you want to get even deeper into your analytics and those of your competition VidIQ is a wonderful resource. They have a free-to-use option, as well as premium paid memberships. VidIQ will help you get even more in-depth into your analytics, keywords, watch time, and more.

It may take time to develop your brand, learn which keywords to use and where to place them, and to track your analytics, but it is well worth your time and will pay off in the end.

Chapter 8: Making a Profit

YouTube is a phenomenal asset for making a profit. Not only can you promote your business leading to more sales, but many people make a business out of their channel itself, and are paid to do so. In this chapter, we will be going over all the ways to can get an income through YouTube. And remember to relate to Chapter 4: Types Of Content to see what videos would work best with the products you want to sell.

AdSense

Google Adsense is the most known way to make money. Once you sign up for the program, Google will place video and text ads on your content, and when people click or view these ads, you get a portion of the profit. However, before you can use AdSense, you have to be a YouTube Partner, which requires you to have a following of at least one-thousand people and four-thousand watched hours within the past twelve months. Even once you reach that, while you will get a bit of profit it won't be that much unless you are getting hundreds of thousands of views.

When you do get paid, you will be paid at the beginning of the month for the previous month's earnings.

Affiliate Marketing

Affiliate marketing works by reviewing or sharing about various products and services with your viewers and then giving them a link to that product or service. If your viewers click that link and buy the product, you will then receive a commission.

One great example is Amazon's Associate program, if someone buys something from your link, you will receive up to 10% in advertising fees. Not only that, but within the next twenty-four hours, if that person buys *anything* on Amazon, not just the product you mentioned, you can receive a commission.

Another affiliate program you can go through is ClickBank, which is the most popular affiliate program to get links through.

The important thing to remember with affiliate marketing is to let your audience know that no matter what you will be honest with them, because if they can't trust that you are telling them the truth, they won't want to watch you. Secondly, legally you must make sure they know it is an affiliate link.

For that matter, if you are doing any affiliate programs, ambassador programs, endorsements, or anything of the like, you legally *must* disclose that you are being compensated.

Affiliate Marketing is one of my favorite ways to make money because it is so passive! You don't have to worry about shipping the products, dealing with the customer service...nothing. This is why affiliate marketing is so powerful and can be used so often.

Ambassador Programs

Ambassador programs are a highly sought after income source on YouTube. A company, for instance, Vitamin Water, will hire you to show and talk about their products.

This helps them humanize their brand and word-of-mouth is one of the most successful forms of marketing. If people trust the YouTuber who is recommending a product, then they are likely to try it.

Google keywords related to your brand with "ambassador program" to try to find some in your niche.

Selling Merchandise

If you create merchandise and show it on your channel such as paintings, tee shirts, hats, or stickers, more people will be likely to see and buy it, especially your loyal subscribers. Just make sure you always include a link in the description and let people know it is there.

There are some great websites out there that you can sell merch on such as Society6, Red Bubble, Merchify, Spreadshirt – there are literally hundreds of options.

Another great option is to sell digital content such as music, information courses, or eBooks.

An easy way to sell your products is by reviewing them or simply at the end of your YouTube videos mentioning where they can get the product (if it relates to the video you have uploaded)

YouTube Channel Memberships

In June of 2018 YouTube rolled out their Channel Membership program. This will enable channels that use it to have viewers sign up for a small monthly fee, most of which will go to the channel owner. The viewers that sign up will receive various benefits such as custom badges, emojis, early access to content, live streams, and other perks that the channel creator is able to decide on.

Promoting Your Brand

If you want to promote your own business and brand that is an option as well. Some great ways to do this is to feature success stories of whatever you are selling, testimonials from people who you have worked with, and show your product so people can fully see what it is and how it could benefit them.

You can also create your own ads for YouTube. The type of ad with the highest success rate is the re-marketing ad. You can have Google Ads target people who have been to your channel, watched certain videos, visited a certain page, viewed a certain channel, and more options. Re-marketing is successful because it targets people who are more likely going to be interested in your brand.

There are many ways to develop a successful income on YouTube, but one of the most important things is to not keep all of your eggs in one basket. Diversify your income streams so that you aren't making just one source of income on YouTube, a little AdSense here, a little ambassador program there, maybe some affiliate marketing. The more sources of income you have, the more you will make, but also if you lose one of them for some reason, you will be okay.

How Payment Works:

When you get paid with AdSense you will be paid at the beginning of the month for the previous month's earnings.

How much you get paid will vary. For instance, AdSense

when paying for click-based payment ads will pay you 68% of the profit that the client is paying to have their ad shown on your videos. So, each time someone clicks that ad you will get 68% of whatever that ad costs. However, different ads cost different amounts, so there are a few hard numbers on this.

Most people don't like to give the number on how much they make with AdSense, however, Pat Flynn of Smart Passive Income shared his numbers. Per 1,000 visits to his niche website, he would make approximately $48 in September.

YouTube Advertising

Using ads on YouTube to promote your channel or business can help you grow.

Getting started with ads is easy, just visit YouTube.com/yt/Advertise to get all of the tools you need. You can pay for two types of ads: one is paying for each time someone clicks on the ad, and the other is paying for each day your ads are displayed.

Most businesses will start with paying about $7, or £6, per day for a local ad campaign.

However, it is better to wait until you have more money coming in from your business before you throw too much money at it. Try holding off on the ads until you start seeing a profit and see that your YouTube channel is growing.

Bonus Tip*: It's always good to leave affiliate links on the equipment you are using for your videos. For example if you have a Tripod and microphone that you got from Amazon. Sign up to Amazon associates and grab the affiliate link for those specific products you use and leave the link affiliate link in your YouTube description below your videos. This is what's called an indirect affiliate link and you can do it with anything. Just make sure you believe in the product you are promoting!

Conclusion

YouTube is the perfect option for those who want to promote their business or create a brand. It gives you the ability to connect with your audience in a way that is nearly impossible anywhere else. Seeing your face and hearing your voice will give people a new opportunity to get to know you, and hopefully, trust you. It also gives you the ability to understand what your audience is looking for, and how to better market yourself.

You can draw people to your social media and website, sell products, and if you are patient, you can make a profit.

While more expensive high-quality equipment can help your production, it is not at all necessary and now more than ever there are inexpensive options that most people already have or can get access to at little cost. This makes YouTube a wonderful, accessible option for those who don't have a large budget to get started and for small businesses to promote themselves.

Now it is time to stop reading and go out and use the tools you have learned. If you use what you have learned here, such as filming, editing, SEO, using your niche to your advantage, and being dynamic, you can be successful and maybe even go viral.

Thank you for choosing YouTube Marketing for Beginners: All the Tools You Need to be a Success! If you found this book helpful a review on Amazon is always appreciated.

www.ingramcontent.com/pod-product-compliance
Lightning Source LLC
Chambersburg PA
CBHW071522210326
41597CB00018B/2858